RECOVERING CRASH OUT

ANTONIA ROYAL WHITMORE

Publack Library Publishing

Antioch, TN

Website: www.publacklibrary.org

Email: info@publacklibrary.org

Crash Outs Only Playlist

Listen on Spotify:

https://open.spotify.com/playlist/6zlSjcqVkbJV6eSYqOQRBJ?si=FcsXE1kzSlmWMVLySUazKg&pi=s0pMA9s-Sbq8m

I'ma Go Crazy: Neisha Neshae
Man Down: Rihanna
Murder on My Mind: YNW Melly
Ring The Alarm: Beyonce
Kill Bill: Sza
Breakin' Dishes: Rihanna
Be Careful: Cardi B
Set it Off: Boosie Badazz
Triggered: Jhene Aiko
Wam Bam: Minaleo
I'll Kill You: Summer Walker
Lord Don't Make Me Do It: Lil Durk
Deep End: Foushee
Whoop That Trick: Al Kapone
Knuck If You Buck: Crime Mob
Hood Bitch: Fam0us Twinss
Sorry: Beyonce
First: KenTheMan
Truth Hurts: Lizzo
Vent: Baby Keem
Never Scared: Bone Crusher
G-Shit: Webbie
Jump: Mystikal
Party Up: DMX

Synopsis

They say I put the "psycho" in psychologist... and maybe they're right.

Once a respected psychologist and leading researcher in women's health, Dr. Meadow McRae found herself on the other side of the locked door—an inmate at Hazelwood Grove Correctional Facility, in Block Crash Out.

They call it crashing out—an explosive, often inexplicable snap. Before Hazelwood, Meadow didn't know the term. Now, she realizes she's lived it.

Inside, surrounded by brilliant, volatile, and broken women, Meadow begins to see what others have missed: a chillingly consistent pattern. These women aren't just impulsive or angry. Many of them share something else—a biological cycle. Now, Meadow is determined to prove what the system refuses to see: that a woman's luteal phase—a hormonally charged window between ovulation and menstruation—could be the silent trigger behind their most destructive decisions.

Released from the prison's hold, Meadow continues her groundbreaking research while facilitating Recovering Crash Out, a curriculum designed to help inmates tame their emotions and reintegrate them back into society.

Chapters

crash out

play the game

the gift that keeps on giving

je nes sais pas

13th reason

green beans

cupid

no regrets

elvis

release date

crash out

Studies show that over 13% of women inmates serve time in federal detention centers due to complications in their intimate relationships. I know for a fact that number is significantly higher.

From my clinical observations and personal experience, more times than not, men sit at the center of women's ruin.

We view it on reality TV, hear it from our girlfriends, and witness it up close and personal as women love their men, support them, fund their dreams, cook, clean, and please them, just to be slapped in the face with infidelity, manipulation, and abuse, the perfect ingredients to unleash a crash out.

I was unfamiliar with the term crash out until I entered the thin walls of Hazelwood Grove Correctional Center, an intimate high-security women's prison located in the bare woods of Maine.

In the professional world of psychology, "crash out" is considered slang, improper English even. We researchers typically use labels like neurotic, disturbed, or psychotic to describe an act performed to seek vengeance on a person or group of people in response to disrespect or hurt. However, I was no longer a professional. I was an inmate.

Recovering crash out

Antonia Royal Whitmore

My career was deemed extinct by peers and colleagues. There was no feasible way to continue my investigation on women's health behind bars, or so we all thought.

Immediately, I recognized my new environment was crucial to the second phase of my research study. I could potentially test how lethal a women's biological cycle was by surveying the women that inhabited Hazelwood Grove Correctional Facility.

I listened as women poured their hearts out to me, disclosing intimate details of their lives and the events leading to their incarceration.

As a result, I used their data to analyze how women's hormonal changes can lead to criminal behavior. The goal was not to exonerate women of their crimes but to emphasize the biological factors that encourage women to act out of their normal, crash out if you will.

The objective of this study is to illuminate the relationship between a woman's hormonal cycle, specifically the luteal phase, and criminality.

The most crucial part of this study is finding an effective remedy and mass education. The public must understand a woman's fight against the threat and fragility of her cycle.

I hypothesize that if an effective remedy is created and our study is empathized by the public, then women will no longer overpopulate prisons, and avoid other consequences caused by uncontrollable biological factors.

While my research is ongoing, I conduct a group therapeutic program at Hazelwood. As documented in my probation terms, it was my duty to create and teach a curriculum that mitigates repeat offenders and helps inmates properly transition back into the real world.

I designed the curriculum to promote accountability, address unresolved childhood trauma, provide health education, and equip participants with emotional, relational, and practical tools for successful reintegration.

Renewed Women, also referred to as Recovering Crash Out, is a fast track to freedom. Inmates are hand-selected by the warden and I to participate in this intervention for a chance at early release. Most inmates dream of the opportunity, but only a few dreams come true.

Upon completion of this program, participants will be immediately granted parole. In the event that participants do not complete this program, they will serve out their entire sentence.

If this program is successful, participants will reintegrate with the necessities to start a new, productive life. Most importantly, they'll have the resources and competence to refrain from entering another lockdown facility again.

These are their stories.

play the game

Four women in matching striped jumpsuits sat in a tight circle, their eyes sharp with boredom as I stepped into the cramped classroom tucked away in the farthest corner of the prison.

It's impossible to ignore the conspiracy theory of the school-to-prison pipeline when the resemblance of a regular classroom and the prison's are identical. A chalkboard, lopsided tables, chairs with engraved doodles, and a tiny stained window facing freedom, lit by a dim light bulb.

I cleared my throat. "Good morning, ladies."

Unsurprisingly, I was greeted with eye rolls and blank stares.

"Let's start with introductions! Welcome to Recovering Crash Out. I am Dr. Meadow McRae, your facilitator and former inmate. Before doing time, I was a rising women's health psychologist in Chicago, researching brain alterations in women during their monthly cycle. That is until an act of reckless rage cost me my freedom.

Now, I use my experience as an inmate and my professional insight to help women outgrow their inmate ideology.

Who would like to go next?"

Recovering crash out

Antonia Royal Whitmore

Rocking back and forth blowing bubble gum, a petite woman, in her late 20s, with smooth brown skin and a low fade broke her silence, "What did you do?"

Redirection was something I'd grown used to working with inmates. "Thanks for volunteering. Tell us your name."

"Ugh, I'm Yvonne. I was charged with theft." "Welcome, Yvonne."

"Ginger. Here for three counts of aggravated assault," a middle-aged woman covered with body tattoos mumbled.

Ginger had the perfect blend of African and Latin features. Full lips and sharp cheekbones with a loose mullet touching the nape of her back. Ginger's edginess was undeniable; underneath her nonchalant act was combativeness.

"Thanks for being here today, Ginger."

"Hi, I'm Chloe here for attempted murder," an adorable girl with clear dark skin and a full afro sprouting from her head, shared.

Braces beautified Chloe's smile, expanding her round cheeks. If you ask me, she looked too young and innocent to be behind bars. But one thing I've learned as a therapist, researcher, and convict is the power of the Halo Effect. A person's beauty, charm, and manners can create a massive illusion of purity.

An older woman in her early 70s sat with her arms tightly folded over her chest. She stared out the small window through her bifocals as her salt-and-pepper locs dangled. "Sonia."

Sonia reminded me of my grandmother— stern and direct.

"Now that we're acquainted, let's review some rules."

Instructions were tricky with inmates. They knew the rules of the prison, but often tested the waters, longing for the slightest inkling of control. Rules were not negotiable in this program. If they are broken, the chance at early freedom is withdrawn.

"Rule number one: Participation is required. Rule two: No tardiness or absences."

Ginger smacked her lips. "Goddamn, we can't miss one day?"

"That is correct. The blank walls in your cell will be there to stare at when you get back from class."

Some of the ladies laughed.

"Keep laughing, and Ima give you something to laugh about," Ginger threatened.

"Rule three: No threats.

Rule four: Tell the absolute truth.

Rule five: What's said in this room, stays in the room.

Rule six: Have all homework assignments completed before class begins."

"I'm not doing this shit." Sonia limped to the correctional officer to escort her back to her cell.

"Does anyone else want to leave before I continue?"

The ladies shuffled in their seats but didn't move. "Your first assignment is to revisit your childhood,"

I instructed.

Ginger leaned on the back of her chair. "For what?"

"Our childhood holds the genesis of the patterns that rule us, the root of our traumas and triggers, but most importantly, solutions to our present issues."

You could hear the rusted water pipes dripping in the corner as each woman processed their first assignment.

"I want you to describe your childhood, your relationship with both parents, or lack thereof, the things you experienced, lessons learned, and how their parenting impacted your decisions in life. Be specific; add as many details as you can.

This assignment requires raw vulnerability. Something you probably haven't been able to explore in this hostile environment. However, it is crucial to your rehabilitation that you connect with the tender pieces of yourself."

"I don't even know if this class is worth it," Ginger whined.

"You don't think you're worth a second chance? If you can give a man a second, third, and fourth chance, you surely can grant yourself the same grace. Don't sabotage this opportunity. See you next week," I dismissed class.

The ladies quickly walked out of the classroom in a single-file line, ushered back to their cells by the correctional officer.

I left the small room and entered the bleak hallway as the familiar smell of bleach, corn chips, and menstrual blood filled my nostrils. The prison always carried different scents depending on your location.

The cafeteria held a permanent stench of old fish grease and pinto beans, and the TV room smelled like feet. I learned early on to hold my breath anytime I entered the bathroom and made a DIY perfume to keep my clothes and cell aromatic.

After a while, every room smelled the same. I unintentionally normalized the prison's stench, forgetting how oppressive and suffocating its chemical-induced air was.

Now, I'm fight to keep down my breakfast every time I step into this facility because of its nauseating ventilation.

I made my way to the warden's office, relieved that the air was less sickening. The warden's small cubicle was trimmed with documents on the floors and tables. "Good morning, warden."

The warden invited me to take a seat. "Meadow! How was your first day of class?"

"Nothing I haven't seen before. Nothing I can't handle. Mrs. Sonia Okoye dismissed herself from class today. I would like to speak briefly with her, if you don't mind."

"I will have the guards let her know you'd like to talk, but she isn't obligated to see you."

"I understand that. I'll be waiting in the visitation room."

I sat at my favorite table in the corner where the murky window allowed an inch of sunlight to enter the prison. At this table I received some of the best and worst news of my life.

"Meadow, Dad died," my big sister, Drue, sobbed.

"You told me he was doing better."

"He was. I don't know what happened. Mom is a wreck. She's overthinking the funeral arrangements and hasn't slept in days. On top of that, some weird guy called and said he was Dad's lover."

"Tim?"

"What the fuck Meadow. You knew about this? You knew Dad was having an affair with a man and didn't tell Mom?"

"She knew. It was obvious Dad was gay."

"Was it as obvious as your husband having an affair and impregnating his mistress?"

"You're stressed, you're grieving, and you should leave," I advised.

Antonia Royal Whitmore

"At least I can leave," Drue bragged before marching out of the prison.

The jingles from Mrs. Okoye's ankle cuffs snapped me back to reality.

She limped to the table and plopped down on the firm stool. "Can I help you?"

"Yes. What caused your early departure from class?"

Mrs. Okoye picked at her nails. "I don't like your kind."

"My kind?"

"Sadiddy motherfuckas who are easily manipulated by the White man. You proudly parade your degrees, failing to realize they've brainwashed you. You know why they call it a master's degree?"

I leaned in forward. "Inform me."

"They've mastered your mind. They've distracted you for so long with their history and indoctrinations that you blindly feed and fuel their agenda. I refuse to participate in your foolishness."

"Mrs. Okoye—"

"Call me Sonia."

"Sonia, you've been imprisoned for decades while politicians, celebrities, and athletes roam free, lacking any repercussions for heinous crimes they've committed.

Recovering crash out

Antonia Royal Whitmore

You're too intelligent to rot in a cell for fear of being indoctrinated. One can only be indoctrinated if they choose to be.

You and I both know life is a game of chess, not checkers. This system is disinterested in women who look like me and you, so play the game, Sonia. Complete the program and enjoy the little freedom you'll have left. With all due respect, your time on earth is limited. If you want to die behind bars, it was nice meeting you."

I left Sonia at the table and gave a brief good-bye to the few correctional officers I grew to like. I quickly exited the prison before I broke down.

After every session, tears rushed down my face from the pins and needles trying to crawl out of my spine. The body has an interesting way of remembering everything.

While serving time, our prison faced a rodent infestation that had the girls fighting roaches and mice more than one another. There was a night I felt something crawling up my back. It took everything in me not to scream; I didn't want trouble with anyone for disrupting their sleep.

I jumped out of bed and stripped completely naked. Two roaches crawled out of my sweater onto the floor. Ever since then, I randomly felt tingling sensations from the inside of my spine. One of the many side effects of imprisonment.

Hazelwood had a unique way of scarring its guests with psychological angst. I've developed an irregular

Antonia Royal Whitmore

heartbeat and I'm constantly met with brain fog that interferes with my thinking and memory. I also suffer from night terrors and experience intense flashbacks. My road to recovery won't truly begin until I am alleviated from the triggers of imprisonment.

I am grateful to have released my title as inmate #36729, even though it means seeking professional help to manage my chronic post-traumatic stress disorder.

the gift that keeps on giving

Ginger strolled into class, eyes narrowed. "You're a hypocrite."

"How so?" I asked.

I felt Ginger's cool breath on my face. "Therapists spend years in school and see many patients throughout their careers, urging them to rise above the cause, be the bigger person, breathe through the pain, and forgive. That peace and light bullshit clearly doesn't work if a skilled professional couldn't take her own advice."

A few years back I'd be devastated by Ginger's insults. Now, I am well versed in inmate bait. "Since Ginger is so chatty this morning, she will start us off with the assignment."

Ginger stared me down. "I'll do what?"

I kept her gaze. "It's very simple. Present your assignment or go back to your cell."

Ginger dragged her feet to her chair. "I'm here to help," I reassured.

Ginger sat quietly for a while, the quietest I'd ever heard her. I could tell she was deep in thought, mentally preparing herself to share unhealed wounds with strangers.

The rest of us patiently waited, listening to the prison's rats scurry across the cemented floors accompanied by the echoes of Yvonne smacking her bubble gum.

"She was my first heartbreak," Ginger whispered. Yvonne stopped smacking. "Who?"

Ginger cracked her knuckles and replied in a dry tone. "My egg donor, the one who accidentally gave birth to me.

Every chance she got, Tamekia reminded me that she never wanted me. I cried when she told me she should have sued the clinic for an unsuccessful abortion.

Tamekia ignored me, like I didn't exist, and only provided my bare necessities. If I wanted a new toy or wanted to attend a field trip, the answer was always the same: no.

She knew I yearned for her attention and intentionally withheld it from me. Her love and affection was exclusively for her male friends, but they often had their attention on me. I wasn't interested in the guys she brought around but she seemed to think so.

Her solution for being "fast" and going after grown men was forcing me to eat large portions of food. She thought my weight gain would prevent her guy friends from lusting over my underage body; when she realized my curves attracted men more, I became her competition.

Tamekia was my first bully. She called me every name in the book and intimidated me with her muscular frame. To avoid her delusional beef, I locked myself in my room. Drawing occupied me.

I planned to go to college, major in art, and become a tattoo artist. Then, I realized I may not live long enough to experience college.

On my first day of 11th grade, I woke up gasping for air. I couldn't stop coughing because of the smoke in my bedroom. I attempted to escape my room, but something was blocking the door on the other side.

My only option was to jump from the third floor of my apartment complex. I stared at the long jump as my room got hotter and smoke filled my lungs. A part of me considered burning to a crisp. No one would realize I was gone, and Tameika wouldn't miss me.

I heard two guys from my apartment complex yelling at me to jump. Jumping three stories into the hands of two strangers fractured my ankle but saved my life.

I was transported to the hospital, where I was evaluated by doctors and interviewed by the police. Temekia showed up at the ER pissed. Instead of asking about my well-being, she warned me that my state insurance better cover my medical bills, or I'd have to get a job to repay her. On the ride home from the ER, she snapped.

Recovering crash out

Antonia Royal Whitmore

"You really are a roach. You don't die for shit. Abortion didn't kill you; the fire didn't kill you; I should crash this motherfuckin' car right now."

When I realized she tried to kill me, I wished I did die in that fire. Death was better than the life I was living.

I longed to be free of Tamekia, but I was a minor with no other support and my father was Casper."

"Casper?" Chloe repeated.

"A ghost. I never seen him before. Tamekia never talked about him, and I never asked. I had no choice but to depend on her while I organized my escape.

Safety was the center of my strategy. I limited my time around her by going to school earlier and attending every after-school program possible. I also slept with a knife under my pillow, and I refused to eat or drink any food in the house."

Yvonne fidgeted with her wrinkled jumpsuit. "Lord have mercy. You thought your own mother would poison your food?"

"Yes. That's partly why I got a part-time job at McDonald's. Free food. I also knew the only way to completely escape Tamekia was to be financially independent.

I worked night shifts, weekends, and holidays, saving every penny I made. To protect my money from Tamekia's thievery, I carved out a small section in my closet to hide my money.

Recovering crash out

Antonia Royal Whitmore

Tamekia was a bitch, but things weren't as bad when she had a man around. I hated seeing her so lovey-dovey with her men, but at least I got a break from the petty arguments and abuse.

I despised the fact that she gave men unconditional love that should have been for me, but what I hated most was how I chased male validation like her.

I was desperate for attention, and Mecca was fishing for flattery.

Chloe politely raised her hand. "Who is Mecca?" "Mecca was one of the guys that helped me escape the fire. I bumped into him at work. I was happy that I

was finally able to thank him for saving my life. "No worries, beautiful, I'm just glad you're ok."

Mecca calling me beautiful shattered the lies Tamekia fed me all my life. I wasn't ugly. His words healed something in me. I clung to them like my life depended on it. His words were kind, but his thoughtfulness lured me in.

He insisted on taking me to school and work, kept money in my pockets, & checked on me to make sure I was good. He was my first experience with safety and protection; the only person I trusted.

My ability to trust was taken away at an early age. Tamekia was creative with finding ways to misuse my trust. Picking me up from school late, many broken promises, lying on me to get out of her problems, and stealing.

17

Recovering crash out
Antonia Royal Whitmore

Something told me to find a better way to hide my money from Tamekia's thievery, but my options were limited. I was heartbroken when I came home from work to see my room ransacked and the small pocket in my closet empty. Tamekia stole all the money I saved from work and the money Mecca gave me.

"If McDonalds is paying you that well, you need to start holding your weight around here. Pay half the rent or get the fuck out my house."

I left.

Mecca saved me once again. He took me in and allowed me to stay in his guest room. Anything I needed, he did his best to provide.

The longer I was around him, the more I fell in love. I knew in my teenage heart that he was my soulmate.

As far as I was concerned, my life was perfect now. I found true love, graduation was approaching, and I finally escaped Tamekia. This was the happiest I'd ever been. Then, Mecca stopped coming home.

I blew up his phone with calls and texts, worried about his whereabouts. Many nights I waited up for him, oftentimes missing school since he was my only ride.

I ate up his lies about how he fell asleep at his dad's house or his cousin's house, that his phone died, or he was so drunk he slept in his car. My naive mind believed him until I found used condoms in his pants pocket.

Recovering crash out

Antonia Royal Whitmore

When I confronted him, he reminded me that there was nowhere for me to go and that real men have multiple women. He told me that if I wanted to stay his favorite girl, I had to allow him to be a man. I did, and grew accustomed to sharing him.

He'd leave me in the middle of the night, and sometimes he brought girls over and made me wait in the living room until they were finished.

My mind was so wrapped around comparing myself to those women, I failed to realize the danger he was exposing me to.

I spent days on Google searching for reasons my vagina was hurting. I felt random bursts of pain that kept getting worse. I didn't know if I was experiencing a yeast infection or something worse because the one thing Tamekia taught me about my coochie was to pop it if I ever needed money.

Open sores appeared on my private area, confirming it was something much worse. Mecca accused me of sleeping with other people and threatened to leave me if I infected him.

The anxiety of waiting for my results had me down so bad I cried for days, and couldn't eat. I don't know why I was so terrified of what my results might say, but I had only been with Mecca.

A few days later, I got a call from the clinic. They told me I contracted chlamydia, mycoplasma genitalium, and herpes.

All I thought about was Mecca leaving me.

Recovering crash out

Antonia Royal Whitmore

"I don't mean to be insensitive," Yvonne cut off. "But what is mycoplasma genitalium?"

Ginger sucked her teeth. "It's an STI with symptoms like yeast infections—pelvic pain, irregular discharge, and painful urination. Many women have it and don't know because most places don't test for it."

"We didn't have stuff like that in my day," Sonia mumbled.

Yvonne was sitting at the edge of her seat, popping her gum. "Correct me if I'm wrong. You knew your partner was sleeping with multiple women, and when you got diagnosed with not one, not even two, but three STIs, you weren't able to put two and two together that he gave those diseases to you?"

I looked over my glasses at Yvonne. "We listen, and we don't judge."

Ginger took a deep breath. "I was 17, freshly out of an abusive home, and deeply in love. I wasn't thinking clearly. My mind was so jaded I planned to kill myself if Mecca left me.

He tested positive for chlamydia and herpes but reminded me that our bond was unbreakable. I was grateful he didn't leave, but the life I envisioned for myself was over.

My dreams of having children were ripped away from me. I wanted so badly to prove to Tamekia that being a good mother wasn't hard, but I wouldn't dare put my children at risk for disease.

Recovering crash out

Antonia Royal Whitmore

Unlike me, disease didn't slow Mecca down. Mecca came and went as he pleased, seducing every woman he laid eyes on.

One night, Mecca came home drunk, slurring his words on the phone, to whom I presumed to be one of his other girls. I pretended like I was sleep to eavesdrop. I'll never forget the chill that ran through my body when I heard Tamekia's voice.

"I bet my daughter can't do you like that, huh?"

"Hell naw. I love some cougar pussy."

I laid in bed paralyzed, listening to Mecca and Tamekia talk about me. I accepted Mecca fucking off with other women, but Tamekia wasn't just other women.

Something snapped inside of me."

"Finally," Yvonne whispered under her breath.

"I was pissed, but I was now a depressed high school dropout with no money. My only choice was to stay with him, no matter what.

I ignored women when they posted him in the "Are We Dating the Same Guy" Facebook groups, I listened as he berated me over and over again, and I waited, with open arms, for him to return after days, even weeks, of disappearing.

He called me his ride or die."

The women in class all shared their disapproval through head nods and deep sighs.

Recovering crash out

Antonia Royal Whitmore

"I found myself forgiving Mecca often, but the one thing I couldn't forgive was Tamekia. To distract myself from the disturbed thoughts that consumed my mind, I returned back to the workforce, against Mecca's orders.

Mecca did not want me to gain financial independence and forced me to rely solely on him for income. I felt less like his partner and more like a sex worker, receiving money only when I put out.

There was a time when he didn't have to ask; I was always turned on by him, but knowing he fucked Tamekia disgusted me. I stopped giving it up and Mecca left to find a *"bottom bitch that could deep throat."* I was relieved but sad he left me right before Christmas.

As my final goodbye, I dropped off the gifts I bought for the family." Ginger's head flew back as she slapped her knee and laughed.

Yvonne bit her nails. "What did you do?"

"I wrapped up the fetus I aborted and gave each of the potential fathers a piece of the fetus. Mecca, his brother Mason, and their father."

The entire group gasped.

"Each gift also came with a handwritten note. His father's note read:

"I don't know if you're the father or the grandfather, but you should book an appointment at the clinic."

Mason's note said:

"You could be the uncle, the daddy, or the brother.

Either way, get your soft dick checked." Mecca's note said:

"Like mother, like daughter. We're keeping it all in the family."

In all my years of therapy, I'd never heard such a story. "If I'm hearing this correctly, you slept with your boyfriend's father and his brother and intentionally infected them?"

"The gift that keeps on giving," Yvonne mumbled to herself in amusement.

Ginger confidently nodded her head. "Yup."

I took a deep breath. "Ginger, I appreciate you for being so raw and vulnerable with us. I have a few follow-up questions for you. The first one is, What have you learned about yourself during your time here?"

Ginger examined the tattoos on her forearm. "I learned that I never had a fighting chance. I was failed by my egg donor. I was failed by the education system. I was failed by the almighty sky daddy and my biological daddy.

I realized why people like me preferred to stay in a place like this. I have friends that are like family who don't play about me. No one can threaten to take away my food or shelter either. This is stability for me.

Stability is so important to me I almost denied the invitation to be a participant in this program. My friends encouraged me to try it so I can get out and pursue my dream of being a tattoo artist."

I jotted a few notes down. "What do you believe will be the biggest challenge for you when you re-enter society?"

"I know my biggest challenge will be staying away from abusive relationships. I've been here for eight years, and I've talked with many girls with similar stories about their man.

Most men are abusive in their own way. Some are emotionally and verbally abusive, others are physically abusive, and they're all liars. I am an abusive man's dream. I will ignore my intuition, and common sense and turn a blind eye to all of his wrongdoings just to be in his presence.

I have this deep hole in my soul that craves male attention, even if it's temporary. The intense desire for love rules my existence and hijacks my intellect."

"Acknowledgment is the first step, Ginger. I have a close friend that has helped hundreds of people with deeply rooted childhood trauma and relationship trauma but—"

"Sign me up," Ginger interrupted.

"But, it's through hypnotherapy," I finished.

"What the fuck?"

"It's completely optional. I do have other resources, but the extent of your trauma can call for extensive treatment."

Recovering crash out

Antonia Royal Whitmore

"Let me think about it."

"Of course. My last question for you is, what does self-sufficiency mean to you?"

"Self-sufficiency means being in control of my own finances and ensuring no one has the ability to dangle my basic needs in my face."

Chloe raised her hand. "Were you able to repair your relationship with your mom?"

"Ironically, her house mysteriously burned up in flames. They found her in her bedroom, burned to a crisp," Ginger awkwardly laughed.

The group fell silent.

je nes sais pas

Chloe broke the silence. "I am prepared to present next."

I loved volunteers. "The floor is all yours."

"My earliest memories involve my nanny, Omorose. My parents hired her before I was born to raise me while Daddy climbed the corporate ladder and while Mommy recovered from the numerous plastic surgeries she underwent after giving birth.

Omorose became my anchor while my parents pursued their own lives. She ensured I was unaffected by my parents' negligence and emotionally supported me with genuine care. She was the epitome of a great mother. If you were to ask me back then, she was my real mother.

When I turned five, my parents announced that Omorose was going away for a while. I was saddened, but I adjusted to her brief absences during the summer and holidays; she'd be back soon, though.

Although I was young and my sense of time wasn't quite developed, I noticed Omorose was gone longer than usual. It wasn't like her to be away this long. Even on vacation, she would call to check on me, but the phones didn't ring.

Recovering crash out

Antonia Royal Whitmore

Every day I stood by the window and waited for her to return, but she didn't. Mommy eventually revealed that Omorose was gone forever. They fired her.

My parents, mainly Mommy, replaced Omorose. I felt like I was being raised by outsiders. Motherhood became overwhelming for Mommy, and I was pawned off to other individuals, once again.

First, there was Mr. Yook, my piano instructor. I saw him every Monday, Wednesday, and Friday for two-hour lessons. Mr. Yook was strict. He allotted me one ten-minute break, and reprimanded me if I played the wrong key. Now, I have arthritis in my left hand at the tender age of twenty-two.

Every Tuesday night, I headed to ballet practice, where I mastered my plié, despite the rich White girls and their mothers who ridiculed my existence.

Mommy couldn't stand the idea of being judged and thought if I lost weight, they would accept us more. Hiring a nutritionist that restricted my diet to small portions of fruit, vegetables, and fish did not stop their judgments. Instead of attacking my weight, my hair became the newest target.

The other girl's mother made complaints with the ballet studio, expressing how my hair was a distraction. Mrs. J., my ballet trainer, advised Mommy to tame my hair before our annual Nutcracker recital.

Rather than defending me or finding another ballet studio, Mommy permed my hair, against my will. I was only fourteen, but I believed in hair autonomy; it was my choice how I wanted my hair to look.

Omorose made sure I loved my kinks and curls, but Mommy unraveled her teachings and lectured me on how appearance garners respect. If I wanted to be someone in life, I needed to look the part.

Perming my hair was the most painful and traumatic experience of my life. It took months before my scalp healed from its many burns and scabs. Although my curl pattern was completely ruined, Mommy was right.

When I returned to ballet lessons with my hair falling to the center of my back, I received the recognition she yearned for. *Jolie pour une fille noire.*"

Ginger glared at Chloe. "What the fuck that mean?"

"It's French for *"pretty for a black girl,"* Chloe translated.

"You speak French?" Yvonne inquired.

"Yes. Mademoiselle Inca taught me French. I spent many summers in her beautiful loft studying France, eating delicious cuisines, and learning the lyrics to my favorite French compositions.

I pretended that French was difficult to learn just to spend more time with her. I didn't fit in anywhere else, and she was my safe space. The White kids in my neighborhood kept me at arm's length, and Mommy alienated me from all of our family.

Recovering crash out

I begged Mommy to spend the summers with my cousins in Houston, but she refused to let me be unsupervised with her family. She didn't tell me the extent of why she was so distant, but made it clear we were prohibited from interacting with them.

Thankfully, she allowed me to visit Mademoiselle Inca whenever I pleased. *J'aimerais qu'elle soit ma mère."*

Ginger sucked her teeth. "Do we need an interpreter or something?"

"I wished Mommy was more like her," Chloe restated. "Mademoiselle Inca was an angel. Her beauty shone from the inside out. She was understanding, nurturing, attentive, and supportive, like Omorose. She saw me as a person; Mommy treated me like a robot.

There was no room for academic error, and my appearance was constantly under review. In order to pass Mommy's daily appearance inspection, I woke up hours before school to complete my extensive skincare routine.

Beauty was the nucleus of our quality time. If we weren't at the hair salon, on an esthetician's bed, or at the nail shop, we didn't talk much, unless she was unhappy.

Mommy scolded me if I broke or chipped a nail and required me to wear gloves to cover my ununiformed hands. She forced me to diet when she thought I was gaining weight and directed me back to the ironing board if my clothes weren't crisp.

Recovering crash out

Antonia Royal Whitmore

While Mommy was big on appearance, Daddy valued connection and network. His favorite line was, "Little girl, it's not what you know, it's who you know." Daddy ensured my network was versatile by enrolling me in every society club, baton, Girl Scout, and sport.

Growing up, I yearned to be a daddy's girl, but as I grew older, I could no longer ignore my evolving resentment. To the world, he was a trailblazing visionary. Personally, Daddy was a corporate junkie, a professional ass-kisser, a sellout, and a lousy father.

Although he was physically present in the home, he was an inactive parent, trading his expected attendance at my games and recitals with gifts and empty apologies, but always reliable for his clients and love interest."

"Being the only child with selfish parents is a different type of loneliness," Ginger validated.

"Well, depending on who you ask, I'm not Daddy's only child. Mommy says I am, but Mrs. J says otherwise."

Yvonne's eyes bulged out of her eye sockets. "Mrs. J., your ballet teacher?"

"Yep. It took Mommy learning about Daddy's affair with Mrs. J to transfer ballet studios. Allegedly, I have a little sister, Aubrey, who's five."

Ginger carefully analyzed Chloe. "I still don't get how someone like you, ended up here. You had it all. Money, materialistic shit, connections, and resources. How the fuck did you manage to ruin your life?"

Recovering crash out
Antonia Royal Whitmore

Chloe twirled her hair. "This was the absolute last place I saw myself being. Life was supposed to be different. I planned to graduate from Spellman University and complete my master's program in a year, to begin my doctoral schedule at Vanderbilt before age twenty-three. I was on track until sophomore year of college. I fell in love.

I met Kayden Jones at a homecoming party hosted at Morehouse College. My roommate didn't want to go alone and begged me to accompany her.

Instead of partying, I found myself a quiet corner to read. Kayden sat beside me and quietly read his book, which happened to be the exact book I was reading, I Know Why the Caged Bird Sings. We bonded over books and became inseparable."

"So he cheated on you with a cheerleader, you found out, and shot him?" Ginger assumed.

"Ginger, we listened to your story; please allow Chloe to tell hers," I warned.

"That's not at all what happened. Kayden was loyal. He was committed to our relationship. The issue arose when I no longer answered my parents' calls and refrained from coming home for holidays.

The freedom I experienced in college was the most independence I'd ever encountered, and I refused to let them ruin it.

After weeks of no contact, my parents made a surprise visit to my school. That particular day

Recovering crash out

Antonia Royal Whitmore

Kaydenand and I were lounging around smoking. When Mommy saw me, she freaked out.

"*Je pensais t'avoir appris mieux que ça!*"

Ginger forcefully grunted. "Is this French class or something?"

"Sorry. She said she thought she taught me better than this. At the time, I thought she was referring to my new habit of smoking. What she actually meant was, she taught me better than being with a Black man."

Yvonne looked Chloe up and down. "But isn't your father Black?"

"Mommy said if she could do it all over again, she'd marry outside her race. Since she can't, she'll make sure I break the generational curse of dating Black and marrying broke."

"So why'd she let you go to a historical black college filled with broke Black men?" Ginger wondered.

"I was allowed to attend an HBCU because Daddy vouched for me and convinced her to trust my decision-making. Mommy reluctantly obliged, as she believed her efforts to keep me from Black influence would drive me away from my new environment. She waited for me to break; she was certain I'd have an unpleasant time at my school of choice, but quite the opposite occurred.

Once Mommy saw who I became unsupervised, she forced me to transfer schools, uprooted me back home, and arranged for me to date her boss's son, Pat.

Recovering crash out

Antonia Royal Whitmore

Pat was your typical mediocre rich White boy. He didn't understand my cultural references and couldn't fathom the many micro-aggressions directed toward me.

In public, he received admiration, sympathy, and validation from his fellow White counterparts while I normalized feeling unwelcome and even insulted.

I complained to Mommy about the uneasiness I experienced, but my complaints fell on deaf ears. She reinforced the beauty of suffering for the right rewards, and I must admit, there were many rewards that were attached to Pat and his last name.

I shared rooms with well-known politicians and A-list celebrities, worked alongside silent billionaires, and even experienced a type of luxury my parents couldn't provide.

Nevertheless, nothing kept my mind off Kayden. I stalked his social media pages and celebrated his accomplishments as if I were there with him. Mommy made it clear that if I contacted him, she would cut me off for good. And even though I entertained the thought of not having to deal with my parents again, I was not prepared for the real world without my family's support. Therefore, I submitted to my family's expectations.

I shape-shifted into the woman Mommy wanted me to be. She coached me on dry laughing, when and how to laugh on cue to boost the egos of dull White men and women. She also trained me how to smile enough to show politeness while minimizing facial lines.

Recovering crash out

Antonia Royal Whitmore

Mommy treated me like I was worthy enough to be her daughter, so I followed all of her instructions.

Everything I did orbited around men to garner their approval. I kept my hair permed and bone-straight at all times, adding extensions to make my hair as long as the other wives' and girlfriends'. I ate one time a day, if at all, and worked out daily.

Things were good. Mommy and I formed a pleasant relationship, I enjoyed the perks of Pat, and I was on track academically.

I just finished my internship in Paris and my third year at university. I wasn't supposed to be home for another three days, but I decided to cut my trip short to surprise Pat. I let myself into his home and waited for him to finish golfing and—"

"And he brought a bitch home, you beat her up, and stabbed her?" Ginger interrupted.

Chloe shook her head. "No. It was worse than cheating. I would have preferred if he did cheat."

Yvonne's eyebrows raised slightly. "What's worse than a cheating man?" "Finding out your partner refers to you as the hard "er" when you aren't around."

Yvonne couldn't close her mouth. "Yea, you're right."

"When he returned home with his two friends, one of them jokingly asked when he'd marry me. His exact words were, *"You know Dad doesn't approve of niggers ruining our bloodline."*

The entire group froze.

"He continued by expressing his disgust for how my vagina looked and how my cocoa butter smelled.

He said having a nigger partner appealed to the family's business ventures, and I was just affirmative action.

Chloe's voice cracked. "I knew I was a placeholder, but it hurt to hear it. Instead of confronting him, I dismissed myself and left. I was done with Pat, and nothing Mommy said could change my mind."

I handed Chloe a tissue to catch the tears that slowly rolled down her face.

"Everything after that was a blur.

You are under arrest for attempted murder. You have the right to remain silent. Anything you say can and will be used against you in the court of law. You have the right to an attorney. If you cannot afford an attorney, one will be provided for you.

My mind did mental gymnastics piecing together who I attempted to murder. Nothing made sense. There must have been a mix-up because I had an alibi.

I just came back home to visit Mommy and Daddy. We arranged a dinner to receive their blessing on Kayden and I's marriage.

Ginger sat upright in her chair. "Did I miss a few chapters or something? When did Kamden get back in the picture? Who did you attempt to murder?"

Recovering crash out

Antonia Royal Whitmore

"His name is Kayden. I'm telling you the story exactly how it unfolded.

The morning of my arrest, Kayden and I made our way from Atlanta to Dallas. This road trip was a quiet one, unlike previous road trips where we'd nerd out singing K-Pop songs, and romanticize about our future. I figured he was just nervous about officially meeting Mommy and Daddy.

We arrived late that evening, where a five-course meal was prepared by my parents' chef Ollie. The atmosphere was tense. I expected dinner to be tough, but not uncomfortable.

No one made eye contact with me, and any time I attempted a conversation, everyone ignored me. I didn't understand why they were so uptight.

Mommy and Daddy were distant, Kayden was spaced out, occupied by his thoughts, and I was anxiously awaiting their blessing on our marriage.

After a quiet and short dinner, Kayden took a jog to get fresh air. I laid down and woke up a few hours later surrounded by police officials.

You are under arrest for attempted murder. You have the right to remain silent. Anything you say can and will be used against you in the court of law. You have the right to an attorney. If you cannot afford an attorney, one will be provided for you.

Mommy and Daddy stood in the corner of the room with shame cemented on their faces as I was ushered out of their home.

Recovering crash out

Antonia Royal Whitmore

Terror swallowed my entire body when I entered the backseat of the police car. The cold handcuffs sunk into my skin, pinching me every time the car hit a bump, confirming that this was not a dream.

As if the officer read my mind, a stocky policeman informed me about my arrest.

"You niggers think because you live with us and got a little change in your pockets you can act any kind of way. We're going to make an example out of you. You could have killed that poor boy and his friends with your idiotic behavior."

"And there it was. As the word "nigger" slipped through his thin lips, my memory from the past five months unlocked. It felt like I was in a hypnotic state, and the word "nigger" freed me from its trance.

Snapshots of crashing my G Wagon into Pat's home, and running him and his friends over, flashed through my mind.

A loud, high-pitched sound escaped Yvonne's mouth. "You put the "crash" in crash out, huh?"

I mistakenly laughed at Yvonne's joke, and the entire group fell out in laughter. Even Sonia cracked a smile. I was typically good at keeping my professionalism, but sometimes I did break character. "I'm sorry, Chloe. I didn't mean to laugh. Please continue."

Chloe took in a deep breath. "It was in the backseat of the police car when a rigid memory of an eerie silence settling over me, muting my environment, memories, and thoughts after destroying Pat's home.

Then I was in Atlanta. Where I'd been planning our wedding for five months. Life with Kayden was the only world I remembered.

Things were great. I was happy, but I couldn't ignore Kayden's sudden distance. He was elated about our life together but, out of the blue, started acting strange."

"Cold feet?" Ginger wondered.

"That's what I thought too. Which explained why he suggested we visit my parents to receive their blessing on our marriage even after we unanimously agreed to elope and stay in Atlanta, away from my parents. Nonetheless, we headed to Dallas."

Ginger gasped. "It was a setup."

"It was. The police were looking for me for five months. Once the private investigator my parents hired found me, Mommy and Daddy reached out to Kayden. He agreed to bring me back to Dallas just as long as the authorities didn't ambush me immediately. They staged our dinner and waited until I fell asleep to notify the police," Chloe outlined.

Yvonne leaned forward. "Let me get this straight. Your White boyfriend called you a nigger, you crashed his house, ran him and his friends over, appeared at your ex's doorstep with no memory, and started a life with him for five months while the police were looking for you? And when your parents found you, they conspired with your fiancée to turn you into the cops?"

"Precisely. Once I was booked at the jail, it was revealed to me that Pat was paralyzed from the waist down, Lyle, his best friend, broke his arm, and Henry, his other friend, ended up permanently blind in one eye."

"Sounds like a case of temporary insanity," Yvonne noted.

"Could have been, but my attorney was no match for Pat's legal team. Being cut off from my family, I had no finances, and my pro bono attorney lacked resources, time, and power.

Fortunately, I built a solid network and called in a few favors. By the end of my trial, I was only convicted of second-degree attempted murder. Very different from three counts of first-degree attempted murder and a laundry list of other nonsense charges."

Ginger was wide-eyed. "Who's all in your network? Annalise Keating? Olivia Pope?" Yvonne fell out in laughter.

I pinched myself on the arm to keep from laughing. Chloe looked confused. "Who are they?"

"Never mind. What happened to you, though?" Ginger pondered.

"It wasn't until Daddy came to visit me that he disclosed I probably inherited dissociative fugue. My great grandmother often blacked out, skipping town where she'd start a new life, under a new identity.

Recovering crash out

Antonia Royal Whitmore

If Mommy found my great-grandmother or when the police returned her home, she'd be unresponsive to her old life with her memory data wiped.

After speaking with a professional, they concluded I suffered a psychotic break at Pat's house, which triggered my dissociative fugue.

I was interested to learn more about my great grandmothers' condition, our condition, and Mommy's experience with it but I haven't seen Mommy since the night the police were called, three years ago.

Daddy felt like he owed me the truth but reiterated that neither he nor she will support me.

Now that I am free from my parents, I spend the majority of my time planning my dream wedding with Kayden. The day after my release, Kayden and I arranged to elope."

"Oh shit, Kamden stayed with your crazy ass?" Ginger wondered.

"Kayden. And yes, I always knew he was the one."

Sonia shook her head in disgust. "The real question is, why did you forgive him after he betrayed you?"

"I didn't blame him for turning me in to the authorities. He didn't have a choice. Kayden hated himself for what he did, but he's been my main support through this experience.

He attends every court hearing, writes me love letters, adds money to my books, and visits me weekly. I love him so much."

Recovering crash out

Antonia Royal Whitmore

Sonia rolled her eyes.

I jotted down a few notes. "Chloe, thank you for sharing your story and giving us a mini French lesson. My first question for you is, how do you feel about the person you were before incarceration, and how do you see yourself now?"

"Je ne sais pas. I don't know who I was back then. Maybe a shadow?

I do know I was lost, forced to tiptoe in life since my steps were heavily monitored by everyone around me. I did so well in ballet because anxiously tiptoeing was my specialty.

Without Omorose's early nurturing and affirmations, my environment would have sucked me up and condemned me to the sunken place.

I was forced to neglect and deny my ethnic being for an empty, superficial way of living. As a result, my self-esteem underwent a significant decline, and I suffered an identity crisis.

Despite living in the safest neighborhoods in Dallas, I struggled with both internal and external safety. Fear had a stronghold on me and did not loosen its grip. But now, I'm finally free."

Ginger laughed. "You're quite literally a prisoner of the state."

"I'm no longer a prisoner to my parents, to respectability politics, or to race and gender roles. I'm free to be myself. To love who I desire."

41

Recovering crash out
Antonia Royal Whitmore

"Where do you see yourself one year from your release date?"

Chloe smiled. "Aside from marriage, I plan to finish university, pursuing African American studies instead of medicine like Mommy wanted.

I aspire to launch a non-profit for girls who grew up like me—rich, connected, but unclaimed by her environment and disconnected from her roots.

I plan to connect with my roots and build a relationship with my estranged family and hopefully gain insight about my great-grandmother.

I've read every book under the sun about dissociative fugue but it lacks the raw voices of survivors and their families. I believe I'll have a better chance of navigating my condition if I confide in family and other diagnosed individuals.

Travel was a big part of my upbringing, and I'd love to bury my toes in Jamaican sand or finally experience the hot African sun kiss my skin."

"Africa does sound nice," one of the correctional officers admitted.

I shook my head in agreement. "Final question. What kind of support system do you think you will need when reintegrating back into society, and how do you plan to create or strengthen that support system?"

"I'm building my support from scratch. I've learned how to be my own support and validate my ideas and decisions, which has helped tremendously with my codependency.

If I reconnected with Omorose and Mademoiselle Inca, I'd feel complete. I've tried searching for them to no avail, as my resources are mighty limited.

As for my parents, I've accepted the reality that I could never be the daughter they hoped for. I wish them the best, but our relationship is forever compromised.

In the meantime, Kayden will continue to be my main support. I don't know what would happen if I didn't have him around."

"Thank you, Chloe. You did great. I have a few support groups in mind that may be of service to you once you're released. There is also a scholarship I encourage you to apply for when you're ready for college."

"*Merci beaucoup.* Thank you so much, Dr. McRae."

I stood for a small stretch. "I think this is an appropriate time for a break. We'll reconvene in 10 minutes."

I slipped out the door to the bathroom to catch my breath. My trembling hands held me up as I doubled over the tiny, rusted sink. The bare gray walls closed in on me.

13th r e a s o n

It was my first day as an inmate. My eyes hadn't adjusted to the lack of color around me. The dull grey walls and striped jumpsuits strained my swollen eyes. Crying didn't change much, but tears were all I could call my own.

My eyelids cradled my tears as I slumped in the crowded cafeteria, poking at my undercooked sausage links. I was met with stares followed by whispers.

Inhale for three, hold for five, and exhale.

Breathing techniques were my first recommendations to patients when they were in distress, but inhaling the scent of undercooked meat and heavy disinfectant would not soothe my distraught body.

"You look like you can use some company," said a young stud with hair slicked back, as she slid into the empty space across from me.

I kept my eyes glued to my sausages. I was too weak for confrontation.

She extended her hand. "I'm Elvis. I conduct orientation for all fresh meat. It won't take long. I know you have better things to do.

Most of the girls in our block stay out of the way, but will always be in your business. We don't fight too much and we look out for one another.

Recovering crash out
Antonia Royal Whitmore

If you need your hair done, go to Ri-Ri. She'll charge you two bags of Hot Cheetos and a king-size Snickers.

JP does nails, but only on Fridays. She doesn't take walk-ins, so book ahead of time.

And never eat breakfast if the lady with the eye patch is in the kitchen. Any questions?"

I shook my head.

"Welcome to Block Crash Out."

I finally looked Elvis in the eyes. "I thought this was block D. I'm in the wrong cell unit."

Elvis laughed. "You're not in the wrong place. This is definitely block D. Inmates call it Block Crash Out because the majority of the ladies that fill these cells are, in fact, crash outs."

I was deeply confused. "Crash outs?"

Elvis shook her head. "A crash out is someone who lets their impulsive thoughts win. It's a person that seeks revenge first and deals with the consequences later."

My researcher's ears perked. "You're telling me a crash out is someone who's willing to throw it all away—her freedom, her future, even her life—in a split-second act of rage or pride," I paraphrased.

"Yup."

Maybe I am in the right place.

Elvis took a bite of her fruit salad. "Most women, probably you too, ended up here because of their 13th reason."

Recovering crash out

Antonia Royal Whitmore

I couldn't keep up with her slang. "13th reason?"

"It's a phrase to describe when a person is at their wit's end. Another way to think of it is the straw that broke the camel's back.

For a lot of women in lockup, that straw was either a man or Mother Nature."

I knew this.

Before my sudden life change, my days were spent behind closed doors diagnosing patients as they unloaded their troubles to me. Relationships were a recurring theme.

A cheating husband reprimanded by his faithful wife. A modern woman being coerced by her narcissistic partner to reject her individualism and submit to him. A fiancée compromising her sanity to keep a man despite the repeated interference of the mother of his children.

I wouldn't dare verbalize or use the term crash out with my patients, but many of them met the requirements of a crash out. Irrational. Careless. Enraged.

When I wasn't defusing and repairing relationships, I conducted research studies in women's health, highlighting reproductive functioning in minority women.

As a woman who lacked knowledge of her anatomy and its functions, coupled with the lack of comprehensive data around menstrual cycles, I developed an interest in exploring the physiological and psychological effects of the female hormonal process.

My colleagues and I spent the last two years interviewing women throughout their hormonal cycle, tracking their mood, food intake, skin modifications, quality of their relationships, and energy levels.

We also collected blood work, examined vitals, and monitored brain activity to compare each hormonal phase.

What we found was that the animalistic part of the brain, the amygdala, was most active during a woman's luteal phase, explaining why women are more primal during this time.

With brain scans and self-reports of thousands of women, my colleagues and I concluded that the luteal phase discretely sabotages women without their knowledge by deeply impacting their quality of life, relationships, and functional decision-making.

Our research population consisted of participants from every age group and generation. One of the many observations I noticed, regardless of age, was that most women weren't familiar with their monthly cycles. To that, I owe racism, sexism, the educational system, and the medical field, for the lack of proper insight on women's health.

The average girl understands she should bleed a few days once a month but remains clueless of the other three stages her body transitions through monthly.

Women are unaware that once the menstrual phase, the bleeding, is finalized, they enter the follicular stage. The two-week period when women feel their best and can take on the world. Every piece of laundry is folded, she's cheerful, and content with life.

Recovering crash out

Antonia Royal Whitmore

Our bodies then turn against us, forcing us to mate during ovulation. Our hormones reach their peak concentration during this time; now we're hot and ready. If women understood the ovulation interval, many unwanted pregnancies would be prevented.

Although ovulation, the releasing of an egg waiting to unite with sperm, only lasts up to 24 hours, women still have a three to five day window where conception is feasible.

While ovulation is flirtatious and sensual, the luteal phase is home to PMS (Premenstrual Syndrome) and PMDD (Premenstrual Dysphoric Disorder). I now refer to this phase as the Luteal Phase Crash Out Syndrome.

Women, and the people around them, can easily identify her luteal phase because she's moody, hungry, and lethargic. Things may get dark with the presence of homicidal ideation and/or suicidal ideation.

Many women attempt, and some succeed, at ending their lives during this phase, and this statistic continues to be overlooked.

As the lead researcher in my study, I was forced to terminate the entire research investigation as my time and resources were compromised by imprisonment. Or so I thought.

Elvis helped me realize that my research was far from over. I quickly recognized that the women who inhabited my cell block were instrumental to the continuation of my analysis.

Recovering crash out

Antonia Royal Whitmore

Researchers and doctors aren't advocating enough for women and their wellbeing, neither are the courts. Just as individuals with mental conditions are often granted leniency and alternative sentencing, women's biological and hormonal realities deserve the same understanding and compassion.

I took it upon myself to test the validity of women's criminality and its relation to our luteal phase. I needed to know how many women really weren't criminals but victims of Mother Nature's wrath, victims of Luteal Phase Crash Out Syndrome.

I already identified my research participants, cell block D, and there were no out-of- pocket costs since I didn't have to pay participants or compensate other researchers.

With Elvis's assistance, the entire cell block was waiting to see me. Once the girls found out I was a certified therapist, they wanted my insight. I was booked seven days a week by women that wanted to size me up and test my credibility, but most were eager to vent about their childhood struggles and relationship problems.

In order for me to be their therapist, relationship guru, or ally, every woman had to comply with my terms and agreements.

First, I needed to know the events that led to their imprisonment, the real story. The secondary requirement was a bit more difficult to acquire, but I needed to identify the stage of their hormonal cycle at the time of their alleged crime.

Recovering crash out

Antonia Royal Whitmore

Fortunately, we all had nothing but time. The girls were eager to talk; I was eager to see what Block Crash Out was all about.

I was nervous initially, but it was like I was back in my office listening to patients.

Ri-Ri was born and raised in Tampa, Florida. She caught her boyfriend cheating with her aunt. She involuntarily committed him to a hospital and sold his social security number and other sensitive information on the dark web.

"Can you believe while I was serving time for straw picking for him, you know, giving guns to felons, that nigga was hunching on my aunty? My momma raised me not to fight family, but I put these paws on that hoe, and that still wasn't enough.

I always been a get-money type of bitch, so I used the videos I found of them fucking and uploaded them to porn sites to make a few dollars. A few dollars turned into a few hundred dollars, every month. Their videos paid my rent.

My bald-headed aunty threatened me to delete the videos, but she wasn't stopping shit. Can you believe this bitch snitched on me and I got charged for revenge porn and assault? Mind you, I'm the victim. She was creeping with my nigga."

Then there was La'Monday, who dated a famous Youtuber. When she discovered her partner was collaborating with a woman she disliked, she responded by deleting his YouTube channel with over one million subscribers, and erasing his NBA 2K players.

Recovering crash out

Antonia Royal Whitmore

I was unfamiliar with the YouTube references, but from what I gathered, what she did was unforgivable.

"You can only flatten so many tires, four to be exact. I broke his windows so much he got them custom-made with a material that is almost impossible to break. He even caught me adding weight-gainer supplements to his smoothies during his weight loss journey. But nothing I did made him act right. So, I hit him where it hurts.

YouTube was his life and main source of income. It took years to grow his following and to become a top-earning Youtuber, but I didn't give a fuck.

I deleted all things related to his content; everything went bye-bye. His YouTube channels, Twitch account, NBA 2K profiles and players, and I broke his laptops. I knew he'd be pissed, but he needed to learn I wasn't to be played with.

I expected to break up and make up like always. He wasn't supposed to call the cops on me and press charges. I wasn't supposed to have a warrant out for my arrest. I begged him to drop the charges, and he blocked me.

I knew he would bounce back quickly. His new Youtube channel was back at 1 million subscribers, and he recovered his Twitch account. There was no reason for him to be mad anymore. He needed to apologize to me so we could continue our life together, but he tried to flex and act like he moved on.

That nigga went live with that bitch I specifically told him not to collab with, and something possessed me to pop up on them.

Recovering crash out

Antonia Royal Whitmore

They were recording at his house by the pool when I pulled up. He tried to shield her from me, but I snatched that hoe up by her loose wig, and threw her in the deep end. I jumped on her back and held her down until the police came. Sis almost didn't make it, and I went viral on their live stream. That's how I got my nickname, little mermaid."

Erica was a former trader on Wall Street, who realized her husband was stealing large sums of money from her, to fund his silent gambling addiction.

Her husband owned a fairly successful bar in downtown Toledo, Ohio, passed down to him from his father. He still decided to steal over three million dollars from her in the span of seven years.

"We shared the same accountant, his brother. They both lied and stole from me for years.

I thought my mother was bitter for how she spoke down on men. I believed she was the problem. That if she was more submissive and more feminine, she'd have a better opportunity to experience a good spouse, like me.

My mother wasn't wrong. Men are sleaze balls and hide their true nature and intention all too well.

I beat myself up for being so damn gullible, but my mother reminded me if I continue to be my own punching bag, men will join the fun. Even though I stopped beating myself up, I was heartbroken for weeks. Out of nowhere, something overcame me. I experienced a calculated fury that had no limits.

I cancelled my ex-husband's business insurance and set his bar ablaze. With no business insurance, there was no insurance claim money, and his bar would only be a fragmented legacy.

His brother had it coming too. I called in a favor, and his brother's stock market trades were sold, and the money vanished without a trace.

I got those lying bastards, and I regret nothing."

Samar, a stay-at-home wife and mother, became distraught after discovering her husband masturbating to her son's pictures.

"In my country, we are not allowed to leave our husbands. Divorce is punished by alienation.

I prayed to Allah relentlessly, asking him to heal my husband from his disturbed mind, but my prayers remained unanswered. I found myself questioning whether my husband's prayers were interfering with mine; it felt like we were in a silent battle for Allah's attention.

Life was good for him. He received a job promotion, and our community respected him—everyone except me. How could I respect a man that violates his own children?

Life was uneasy for me. I kept my children close, but that didn't replace the guilt and shame I felt for keeping them around that monster. My mind wasn't going to rest, so I went to my parents seeking counsel. They reminded me that Allah makes no mistakes and advised me to be a supportive wife.

When I caught my husband peeking through the bathroom door, watching my son undress, I knew I could no longer wait for Allah.

Recovering crash out

Antonia Royal Whitmore

Something swept over me; I didn't feel like my normal self when I poisoned my husband's food. I calmly watched him struggle to breathe, and struggle to move until he fell to his demise.

Now I'm here, at peace, knowing my children are safe with my sister. I forgave my late husband and my parents, but my healing did not come with amnesia."

Dove, a self-proclaimed high priestess from New Orleans, defended herself from her partner after a botched conjuration.

"When I consulted with my ancestors, they gave me specific instructions. They told me what tools to use to ensure Jeremy would be my divine masculine in every lifetime.

I filled the iron with my urine and ironed his clothes to ward off any potential love interest, hoping that'll stop him from cheating. Oddly enough, the cheating worsened.

I consulted with my ancestors time and time again to ensure he fully commits to me, but their advice wasn't working. I needed something more effective.

I devoted my time to learning blood magic. Any food I made was contaminated with my menstrual remains, and we regularly participated in blood intercourse to strengthen our bond. I completed the ritual with a jar containing both of our blood submerged in honey, sealed with a purple candle.

My ancestors were unhappy with my practice and warned me to undo my spell, but I got the results I wanted.

Recovering crash out

Antonia Royal Whitmore

Jeremy started coming home from work on time, he stopped cheating on me, and proposed. Progressively, Jeremy became obsessive. It was cute at first; having a man be devoted to me was all I ever wanted. I loved his obsession but hated his control. I couldn't go anywhere without his attendance or permission, not even a jog around the block.

I returned home from a short jog one day and was met with Jeremy's rage. He was pissed I didn't invite him on my jog.

I was used to his yelling and empty threats, but this time he wrapped his hands around my throat. I managed to grab the hammer on the hallway table and knocked him across the head.

My ancestors mocked me for my foolish practices. They punished me by refusing to help resurrect Jeremy or conjure his spirit.

I took matters into my own hands and tried to kill myself to spend eternity with him in the afterlife. My ancestors refused to let me die; they said my work in the physical realm wasn't finished."

After interviewing over two hundred women, I was able to confirm that at least 16% of those women were somewhere in their luteal phase at the time of their alleged crime.

Roughly 68% of the women I surveyed disclosed that they feel an involuntary internal switch that occurs every month around the same time. During this time, they experience character flaws, where they say and do things out of their ordinary and struggle with regulating their emotions.

I must highlight the endless list of factors that contribute to and influence neuroticism and criminal-like behaviors—the most common factor being underlying mental health conditions.

35% of my research participants suffer from at least one mental health condition, most being untreated and undiagnosed.

I knew from the beginning that not every woman would be a victim of Luteal Phase Crash Out Syndrome, but my data was confirming a distinct relationship between women's criminality and their biology.

I was fairly happy with my research results, but there was still a missing component. The remedy.

Effective remedies will help numerous women minimize their monthly turmoil and ultimately depopulate women's detention centers, but true remedies were few and far between.

The best solution for Luteal Phase Crash Out Syndrome is staying away from men.

What I've learned from speaking with women is that romantic betrayal is a trigger for unraveling. Combine that with women's monthly internal conflict, and chaos is inevitable.

Unfortunately for women, men are masters of betrayal. They understand the psychological, and spiritual damage betrayal causes and the danger it holds for all parties involved. Men use betrayal to meticulously control women and feed from their energy.

All the while, women continue to be ruled by their childhood dreams and societal conditionings of a fairytale happy ending, white picket fences, or the Bonnie and Clyde ride-or-die illusion.

Women gravely underestimate a man's willingness to shamelessly destroy and deceive. This unrealized truth has cost many women their freedom, their sanity, and their lives. As far as I'm concerned, any woman that steers away from men, will thrive at their highest.

There are other interventions that may potentially limit crash out symptoms, including taking Pepcid AC to stabilize mood and creating a list of effective coping skills to regulate the nervous system.

Deep breathing and journaling were my personal coping skills of choice, but they weren't enough to balance the adverse effects from internalizing the stories and trauma of the hundreds of inmates I interacted with.

If I had known I'd suffer from PTSD, I would have approached my research differently.

Cold water to the face brought me back to reality.

green beans

"Yvonne, would you like to share your assignment?" I resumed class.

Yvonne bowed her head and closed her eyes. "Our Father who art in heaven, hallowed be thy name. Thy kingdom come. Thy will be done on earth as it is in heaven. Give us this day our daily bread. And forgive us our debts, as we forgive our debtors. And lead us not into temptation, but deliver us from evil. For thine is the kingdom, and the power, and the glory, forever. Amen."

Yvonne opened her eyes and popped her bubble gum. "I'm here because I disobeyed God.

When I was a girl, my foster mother warned me to eat my green beans. I hated green beans; well, I just hated the way Mrs. Winifred made them.

"*Everything God made is good,*" she preached. But her green beans weren't. They left a metallic aftertaste, like battery acid that lingered on my tongue for hours.

Anytime green beans were on the menu, I stuffed them in my pants pocket when she wasn't looking and threw them away in my room.

It all started when I told Mrs. Winifred I wasn't hungry because I ate pizza from my school's pizza party. She told me God was going to punish me if I didn't eat my food and placed a plate filled with soggy green beans, rice, and pork chops in front of me. Luckily, the one lady from church stopped by so she didn't catch me stuffing my pockets with green beans.

When I made it to my bedroom, someone whispered in my ear, "*God gone getchu for whatchu done.*" No one else was in my room.

I was terrified but didn't tell Mrs. Winifred what happened to protect my secret about the green beans; I just pretended like nothing ever happened. And for a while, that actually worked. Until I experienced another episode a few months later.

I stared at the burnt green bean casserole on my plate. My plan was to accidentally drop the plate on the floor, but before I could, a swarm of murmurs filled my head. Mrs. Winifred was right; God did punish me.

My hands were shaking so badly, it was impossible to hold my fork properly. I managed to eat all my casserole, but the voices didn't stop this time.

"What were your voices saying?" I asked.

"In the beginning, the murmurs were indistinguishable words and phrases that circulated in my mind. The first time I heard a clear message was when Cyrus told me to harm our dog, Rico.

"Is Cyrus one of your voices?" Chloe asked.

"He's the ringleader and he hates being ignored. His demand to hurt Rico started off as a faint whisper. Days of trying to ignore Cyrus turned his whispers into belligerent screams. I tried using music and headphones to drown out his wailing, but he left me rocking in a fetal position covering my ears until I gave in.

While the house was asleep, I found matches in the kitchen drawer and took Rico to the bathroom. Tears were blinding my eyesight, and my heart was bound to leap out of my chest, but Cyrus didn't care.

I lit a match and became consumed with its warmth and myriad of colors. My admiration for the flame saved Rico's life. Mrs. Winifred burst into the bathroom right before I lit Rico's fur on fire. I had no choice but to confess to everything. The green beans, the murmurs, and Cyrus.

She frantically made phone calls trying to figure out what to do with me. That one lady from church came over and covered my head in holy oil while speaking in tongues.

I was instructed to talk directly to the demons that possessed me and cast them out. I told Cyrus to leave me alone, but he told me he wasn't going anywhere."

Chloe was wide-eyed. "Is Cyrus still around?" "Well, for a period of time, all of my murmurs were gone. Mrs. Winifred finally put her beliefs to the side to take me to a psychiatrist, where I was diagnosed with schizophrenia.

They suggested my schizophrenia was passed down from one of my parents, but we were unsure since I was an orphan.

Recovering crash out

Antonia Royal Whitmore

I was prescribed antipsychotic medication, and the murmurs slowly began to fade. Medication and religion saved me.

Despite the stigma, I lived a fairly normal life. I graduated from high school, enrolled in community college, and dated Pastor Lonnie Williams. He wasn't the most handsome man, but he was a man of God, my man of God.

Mrs. Winifred suggested I confide with Lonnie about my diagnosis before things got too serious, but those conversations never went well. Anytime I told a man about my diagnosis, they distanced themselves from me.

I was already in love with Lonnie and couldn't bear a heartbreak, so I held off the conversation as long as I could.

One day, he picked me up for our weekly date. I was so excited to go to the aquarium I almost forgot to take my medication. Lonnie carried a strange look on his face as I swallowed my pills and chugged a glass of water. I just knew this was the end of us.

To my surprise, Lonnie asked to pray for my condition. His prayer was different from the time that one lady from church prayed over me. This was intentional; it was intimate. Every word he spoke marinated in my soul. I felt it in my heart that God would remove any demonic spirits from within me.

During prayer, God told Lonnie that I was his kingdom spouse and I never have to take antipsychotics again. Lonnie asked for my hand in marriage and disposed of all of my medication.

Ginger shot Yvonne a perplexed look. "I know you did not let some random man convince you to stop taking your helpful antipsychotics."

Yvonne sighed. "I did, and the murmurs came back with a vengeance almost immediately. My own voice got lost in the sea of voices that resurfaced. New voices appeared, old ones expressed their grievances, and Cyrus was back for blood.

Cyrus was self-destructive. He didn't miss a chance to assert his dominance over me. Anytime I got behind the wheel, Cyrus insisted I crash my car. I cut back on all driving, unless it was to church, but driving to church eventually became complicated too.

I was headed to Sunday service when Cyrus's voice boomed in my head, demanding I drive off the bridge. I started praying immediately, like Lonnie told me, but Cyrus was relentless.

I felt big, cold hands latching over mine, guiding me off the road. Then BAM. I ran into a tree.

By the grace of God, the car suffered minor damages, and no one was injured. To ensure my safety and the safety of others, Lonnie chauffeured me everywhere."

Ginger rocked on the hind legs of her chair. "You didn't think this was a good time to get back on your meds?"

"Of course. I even brought it up to Lonnie. He saw my symptoms worsening but reminded me that our God is a healer and no wife of his will use medication.

I understand the stresses of caring for someone with mental struggles, but I didn't expect Lonnie to become distant. He left me stranded in the house and only took me to church and Mrs. Winifred's house.

Mrs. Winifred suggested I give him a child to spice our marriage up. I quickly dismissed that option and shared my concern about passing my condition down to my children. What I didn't tell her was Lonnie and I had only been intimate once, during our honeymoon, several years back. Lonnie believed semen retention kept him closer to God, which eliminated our romance.

"He gay ain't he?" Ginger speculated. "Was I that blind?" Yvonne considered. Ginger shook her head.

"I knew something was off with Lonnie, but I couldn't put my finger on it. I attempted to confront him on his sneaky behavior, but he called me crazy.

I wept to God in prayer to save my marriage, and after fasting and praying, the Holy Spirit sent me Martha."

"And Martha is?" Ginger asked.

"Martha is one of my avatars. She's my voice of reason and highly respected by the other murmurs. She helped me get to the bottom of my suspicion of Lonnie.

Martha instructed me to follow Lonnie to his weekly minister's meeting. Several months had passed since I sat in a driver's seat, but I knew I was safe; Cyrus and I made amends.

I tailed Lonnie to a motel and was surprised to see Youth Minister Greg open the motel door and tongue down my husband."

Ginger hysterically laughed. "He wasn't completely lying. He did have a meeting with a minister."

I was growing impatient with Ginger. "Ginger, let her finish."

"I didn't mention what I witnessed at the motel and continued to be a supportive wife despite our estranged relationship. My connection with Lonnie was nonexistent, but the bond I formed with my murmurs was indestructible.

I finally stopped being ashamed of my condition and accepted my avatars as a part of me. In return, they protected me and avenged any wrongdoers. My murmurs didn't even allow me to feel bad when God punished Lonnie.

Our church pressed charges on him, and he was arrested for theft."

Ginger uninterestedly picked at her fingernails. "A gay thief thought he would make it to heaven?"

"Well, he was the overseer of the church's finances, responsible for counting and depositing all money into the bank. Our senior pastor decided to conduct a financial audit and realized that over $250,000 was missing."

"He was using that money to fund his minister meetings?" Ginger inquired.

"Allegedly, Lonnie didn't steal the money. His assistant did. Instead of completing his duties as the chief trustee, he delegated his role. His assistant was responsible for collecting all the church's money and depositing it into the bank."

"You were the assistant?" Chloe guessed. "Cyrus was the assistant," Yvonne corrected.

Ginger cracked her knuckles. "What did Cyrus do with the money?"

Yvonne looked out the small windowpane. "He anonymously donated a large sum of money to Planned Parenthood."

"Giving the Lord's money away to an abortion clinic is diabolical," Ginger admitted.

"Diabolical is being a homosexual pastor and having affairs with other pulpit honorees," Yvonne snapped.

"How much you keep?" Ginger pried. "I didn't keep any," Yvonne admitted.

"How much did Cyrus keep?" Sonia broke her silence.

Yvonne smiled. "That's for him to tell, not me."

"Well, bring Cyrus to the front. I've got a few questions to ask him," Ginger suggested.

I shot Ginger a stern look. "Ignore Ginger."

Yvonne shifted in her seat. "Eventually, God spoke to me and demanded I repent."

Ginger shook her head. "Dummy."

"I expected Lonnie to be upset, but I wasn't prepared for him to abandon me. I hadn't even taken my mug shot before Lonnie filed for divorce. I couldn't believe he broke his vows—for better or worse.

I was surprised Lonnie divorced me and felt utterly betrayed when the church divorced me too. My church family didn't visit or even pray for me after the years of service I devoted to them.

I attended Bethel Missionary Baptist Church as a teen. I held positions on the usher board, sang in the choir, and served as the president for the district committee.

Christians can be some of the most unforgiving and judgmental people. Their abandonment hurt worse than my parents' disownment, and I retaliated by exposing Lonnie and the church.

Pictures were sent to pastors' wives and local newspapers of Lonnie and his multiple lovers in compromising positions. I knew what I did was wrong, and every night I pray that God forgives me of my sins. I also pray God delivers Lonnie from the spirit of homosexuality so we can remarry once I'm released."

Recovering crash out

Antonia Royal Whitmore

Yvonne looked me directly in the eyes. "Just to be clear, once I'm finished with this program, I'm being released, right?"

I knew if Yvonne were to be released, it would be to a psychiatric facility or a group home. She made it abundantly clear that medication was not an option for her which makes her a risk to herself and society.

"Well, let's take it one class at a time, Yvonne.

Thank you for sharing your story with us.

To finish your assignment, think of a moment when you felt proud of a positive decision you've made here."

Yvonne took a moment to think. "That moment is every morning when I cheek my meds to show God I am a true believer of his word and healing power."

Freedom is further than she thinks. "You're cheeking your meds?"

Yvonne proudly nodded her head. "If I take them, I'm proving to God and Lonnie I'm not a believer."

Ginger sucked her teeth. "Are you kidding me right now?"

Yvonne put her head down, using her shoe to play with a dead roach on the ground. "Honestly, I wouldn't know what to do without my avatars. They're like mini disciples to me. I can't just neglect them."

In Yvonne's defense, it's possible for individuals with chronic mental health conditions to subconsciously view their condition as safety. Some individuals don't know a life without their mental symptoms and naturally choose a familiar life, with their condition, over an unfamiliar life, without their condition.

Although Yvonne may not be an imminent threat, psychosis is unpredictable even with meds. Her refusal of medication will promise her numerous trips to psychiatric wards, jail cells, or worse.

"What kind of environment will you need to thrive, and how can you create that for yourself?"

"'Long as I got King Jesus, I don't need nobody else. I'm going to find a new church home and become a good and faithful servant."

I took a brief moment to review my notes. "Thank you again, Yvonne."

From the corner of my eye, I felt Ginger staring me down. "When will we hear about the infamous Cupid?"

Out of the many years I'd been facilitating this program, I'd never had someone call me by my inmate name, Cupid.

cupid

I took a deep breath.

"I was born a professional archer, inherited from my father and his father. I lived and breathed bows, arrows, and targets.

Growing up, my targets often consisted of my sister Drue's head or annoying classmates. The same classmates that fought for me to be on their team in gym class because precision was beneficial in every sport.

My accuracy landed me a scholarship to compete in collegiate archery, where I soon understood archery could only be a hobby. My focus switched from sports medicine to psychology.

When I wasn't hitting targets, I found myself people-watching, formulating hypotheses about my environment, and conducting surveys with friends and family about whatever topic interested me.

During my Master's program, I fell deeply in love with my African American Women Studies course, and eventually my professor.

Ginger's eyes were glued on me. "This is getting good already."

"I became Professor's aide, along with other things, and a year after graduation, we were happily married.

Recovering crash out

Antonia Royal Whitmore

Our marriage was fun. We developed several research studies and surveys in pursuit of helping our community. We spoke at conferences, sharing our findings and recruiting like-minded scientists. I was content with life. He wanted more.

Professor expressed how excited he was to start a family. His ultimate desire was to be a father, and soon he'd find out I couldn't fulfill that dream of his.

A family held zero interest in me. As a little girl, I broadcasted my apprehensiveness for children and was met with disbelief. I was told time and time again I would change my mind once I got older. I doubled down on my stance on a childless life by getting my tubes tied. There was more to life than being someone's mother."

"Like being a prisoner?" Ginger snarked. I laughed. "Like being a researcher."

Chloe raised her hand. "Did you tell your husband the truth?"

"There were several times I wanted to come clean, but each time my airwaves tightened and no words came out. I thought about how I would respond if the shoe were on the other foot, and I refused to ruin his image of me.

I led him to believe I was trying to conceive. I pretended to visit reproductive specialists and drank teas to increase my fertility, knowing they wouldn't work.

When I finally decided to confess, the betrayal almost cost me my marriage. He refused to sleep in the same room as me and limited his interaction with me at work. After months of pleading, he reluctantly agreed to marriage counseling.

The efforts of therapy slowly mended our relationship until my father became terminally ill with stage 4 lung cancer.

My father was my role model; I fell in love with archery through him. There was nothing I wouldn't do for my hero, including letting my marriage drift away.

When he fell ill, my world shifted entirely. I poured every ounce of myself into caring for my father—never missing a single doctor's appointment, sitting beside him through every grueling chemo session, and becoming a steady presence he relied on.

When the burden of caretaking became too much for my mother, I stepped in full time, holding my family together as we watched the strongest man we know wither away.

One night, we rushed my father to the emergency room for hemoptysis. He couldn't stop coughing blood.

In the waiting room, I spotted Professor down the hall walking into a patient's room. It was normal for him to check on his patients or participants that may have ended up in the hospital for whatever reason.

At that time, I hadn't seen him in over a week. He periodically checked in on my father, but I missed him and needed his comfort.

Recovering crash out
Antonia Royal Whitmore

I waited outside the room he entered until I heard a female voice say, "He looks just like you."

"Oh no." Yvonne sighed.

"I invited myself into the room to identify the woman. I was surprised to see him sitting at the edge of the bed holding a baby with his former student, my former classmate.

I gave my congratulations to both of them and reassured him I'd have divorce papers signed so he could start the family he always wished for.

He tried to apologize and explain himself, but I was in a daze; too much was happening too fast. My father was dying, my marriage was over, and my cycle was starting soon."

"Periods are chaotic enough. I can't imagine how you felt with the additional weight of betrayal and grief," Chloe reassured.

Yvonne nodded her head in agreement. "Amen."

"My father was finally able to discharge from the hospital, and my mother suggested I take some time to myself.

I used that time to pack my belongings while Professor was away on a trip. As each day passed, a new wave of intense anger filled my heart. Anger at cancer. Anger for my marriage. Anger toward Journey. I disagreed with displacing anger toward the mistress. However, this time was different. Journey was my nemesis, and Professor knew that.

Recovering crash out

Antonia Royal Whitmore

Journey and I shared every class together the entirety of our Master's program, and from day one, we bumped heads. Her energy was off; she was slimy and sneaky, and her high-pitched voice made my skin crawl.

She secured her master's degree by cheating and relying on classmates in group projects. You could count on her to produce not one original idea; plagiarism was her thing. So was promiscuity.

After she caught Professor and I in his office in compromising positions, she took an interest but failed at seducing him. She was determined to have Professor but he didn't budge. He kept things professional with her and constantly turned down her advances.

After graduation, I thought she was out of our lives forever. I hadn't seen or heard from her in years, but I wanted to speak with Journey, face to face, woman to woman.

The group was silent, all eyes on me.

"I sent her a text from my husband's burner phone to stop by. I only wanted to talk, to get a timeline on how the affair transpired.

I anxiously waited for her arrival, rehearsing what I'd say to get the closure I needed. She arrived at my home, and just as I opened the door, she used a key to let herself in. It was unclear if my period was exacerbating my emotions, but I was livid.

I assumed their fling was a seamless affair that resulted in an unplanned pregnancy. Considering that I assumed their fling was a seamless affair that resulted in an unplanned pregnancy. Considering that Professor gave his mistress a key to my home meant they were serious.

She was surprised to see me but eager to gloat.

She was surprised to see me but eager to gloat. "Yes, he gifted me a key to your house. I mean my

Anger paralyzed me.

"A few years back I bumped into Professor at the grocery store. He looked so damn pitiful I invited him for a drink. I was shocked he agreed since you put a tight leash on him. One thing led to another, and he started seeing me every weekend.

He told me about your broken pussy, how your womb was too weak to bring life into this world, so I took it upon myself to give him a child."

"Whoosh. I released my arrow, and it pierced Journey's shoulder. She was lucky I hadn't used my bow and arrow in a while. I grabbed another arrow to finish the job, but my sister pulled up in the nick of time."

Yvonne smacked on her gum. "How did your arrow get in your hand?"

I ended my story time. "That is all I am willing to share."

In group settings, it is easy to cross the line of professionalism. These women needed to understand I was not their equal. My job was to give them enough information about me to build trust and solidify my credibility. Their rehabilitation relied on my ability to be relatable enough for them to internalize the guidance and education I share.

"Cupid fits you well." Ginger admitted.

"You put the psycho in psychologist," Yvonne whispered.

I'd heard many witty remarks from the ladies in this program, but that was my favorite.

Chloe raised her hand. "What happened to your ex-husband?"

Truth be told, I didn't know, and I didn't care. What I did know was that I was happily married.

"Maybe we can discuss that another time. Sonia has been patiently waiting to share her story with us.

no regrets

Sonia shuffled in her chair. "Born in the early 50s, I was tightly hemmed in by the edged stitches of Jim Crow and poverty. We were poor, but we maintained.

Mama died during labor with her eighth child, and Daddy died a few months later from a broken heart. It was now time for me to mature and care for my family at the ripe age of ten.

My seven siblings and I moved in with my mama's sister, Aunt Rose, her four kids, and their alcoholic father.

We filled their small two-bedroom cabin to the brim. There was no personal space or privacy, but we sure figured out how to stay out of Uncle Clyde's way when he got drunk.

The body heat was appreciated during the winter, but the girls were quarantined outside in the summers when we were menstruating.

Our cycles synced together, and with no air conditioning or fans, the house carried a foul stench. The girls slept outside on dead grass to manage the home's odor. We hated being out back, but the mosquitos had a field day with our blood.

Recovering crash out
Antonia Royal Whitmore

Aunt Rose pulled me from school when I was fourteen and took me to work with her uptown, cleaning white folks' houses.

I was excited to work. Mama told me to have my own money, and now I was finally able to. I swept, folded laundry, mowed the lawn, cooked, and even massaged Mr. Hilton's feet, all for $3 a week.

I asked Aunty Rose why she didn't demand a raise, and she told me I needed to be grateful that I was able to work. I was grateful because I understood uneducated black girls struggled to find and keep employment. That didn't negate the fact that we needed better pay.

Our labor as women makes the world go round. I witness women involuntarily give their labor to society. They labored children, labored for men, labored to feel worthy, and all to be cast as an object?

It behooved me that the women who complain about the broken system internalized that same system's hatred for women and bestowed its exact misogynistic, patriarchal bullshit on their young.

Everybody didn't have a Mama like mine. She told me a closed mouth don't get fed and reminded me that if I remain silent about my pain, folks will say I enjoyed it.

Mowing the lawn on a hot July day had me more fancy than usual. I marched to Mrs. Hilton's room and asked her why she only pays me $3 a week. She informed me that she actually pays me and my aunt $50 a week each.

I didn't believe words. Mama always told me to ask for proof. Sure enough, Mrs. Hilton's balance records showed she gave my aunty $100 a week.

I learned early on that the world will use and mistreat you for fun. In my gullible young mind, I considered family to be an exception. When Aunt Rose stole from me, I knew I was on my own.

That night, I slid into her bedroom and woke her up as she stared deep into her shotgun's barrel.

Ginger laughed. "I knew you wasn't to be fucked with."

"I made her give me all her money. I left that house and never looked back."

"You left all of your siblings?" Chloe wondered. "They've been abandoned all their life. Mama left them, Daddy left them, and I was just continuing the cycle. I knew my sole purpose on earth wasn't to be a caregiver, but I couldn't escape it.

By the age of eighteen, I was married and pregnant with my second child. My husband was a manager at a car wash, and I was a stay-at-home mother, bored out of my goddamn mind.

Every day was the same. Crying kids, a distasteful husband, dirty dishes, loads of laundry, routinely cooking, rinse and repeat. I was so young, but my spirit aged poorly. I went unnoticed, overshadowed by my servitude. Riot was the only person that ever made me feel seen.

Ginger doodled on her arm. "What kind of name is Riot?"

"He got his nickname after starting one of the biggest revolts Detroit witnessed after a local pig murdered his brother."

Chloe gasped. "My neighbor had a farm. I had no idea pigs were that vicious."

"Pigs, as in police, the law. Riot avenged his brother's death, backed by hundreds of other Black men and women. They stalled a main bus stop in a predominantly white neighborhood, and when the law arrived, all hell broke loose.

I watched as the news covered this story but never thought I would partake in the revolution.

Riot and I met one night in a grocery store parking lot. I was having car trouble, and he offered a hand. In exchange for the maintenance on my car, he asked me to attend a meeting with the Black Stone Coalition.

He said their group formed plans to unite our people, practice group economics, and fight against the racial injustice taking place around the country.

I didn't know anything about the Black Stone Coalition back then, but the way his eyes lit up when he spoke enticed me. After attending their next meeting, I committed to the Black Stone Coalition life, alongside Riot.

Recovering crash out

Antonia Royal Whitmore

Ginger balanced on the hind legs of her chair. "You left your kids, huh?"

Sonia shot a death stare at Ginger that made her sit on all four chair legs.

"I never understood why more women didn't leave. Leave their husbands, their kids, and their jobs. Women and suffering aren't synonymous. Men leave at the first sight of discomfort, guilt-free, so did I.

Protesting made me feel alive. Believe it or not, this was the first time I experienced joy. The sound of other men and women chanting in unison ignited my soul. I felt my ancestor's protection as I defended myself from the cowards in blue. Jail time was a minor consequence for a greater cause.

I wish more women tasted the freedom of not being bound by children, societal norms, gender roles, or an unimpressive man.

As much as I was opposed to relationships, I chose to commit to Riot. I wasn't forced by the government or pregnancy; he was something I wanted.

Our relationship leaned more on shared values of the Coalition and companionship. There were times I didn't see him for months, even years, because he or I was imprisoned or away assisting other Coalition chapters around the states. No matter what, resilience led us back to one another.

The more resilient our coalition grew, the stricter our jail sentences became. The larger we were in numbers, the easier our deaths were ruled justifiable.

Recovering crash out

Antonia Royal Whitmore

Our comrades were being buried and imprisoned faster than we could rebuild. The Coalition finally dispersed when the FBI infiltrated our assembly. Mistrust plagued our organization until there was no organization.

One person I never doubted was Riot. I stayed by his side, traveling occasionally and joining organizations to educate our people on political power.

After many years of protesting, fighting, and organizing, I was hit with conviction. I'd been demanding the government respect, accountability, and justice when I refused to grant my children those exact things. I mastered the art of recruiting, organizing, and community but abandoned my own family.

With this newfound conviction, I tracked my children down, but my ex-husband dismissed my plea to re-enter my children's lives. I also attempted to rekindle my relationship with my siblings. Some were excited to hear from me; others didn't even remember me.

At the end of the day, I don't regret any of my decisions. If I conformed to the traditional life as a woman, an early grave was inevitable.

I missed my children dearly, but I was content with the life I shared with Riot. Unlike my siblings and children, there was no resentment toward him when it came time to care for his dementia.

Recovering crash out

Antonia Royal Whitmore

Yvonne swayed side to side in her seat. "Dementia is a disheartening disease to manage. Mrs. Winifred was diagnosed, and that was the saddest thing I ever experienced. She was so mentally impaired."

"And a fragile mind can't continue to carry the weight of big secrets. As Riot's dementia progressed, he unintentionally began confessing his faults.

He started referring to me as Lara, but Mama ain't name me no Lara. I verified several Lara's that he knew, that we both knew, but I didn't understand why he called for them.

He went from calling me Lara to asking for his son, Robbi Jr. When we met, Riot was a bachelor, and we agreed to have no kids. I knew Riot wasn't always faithful, but I didn't think he'd hide a child.

I was completely blindsided by his secret child, but my feelings were irrelevant because Riot's health was quickly declining.

I attempted to gather information from Riot on the mysterious Lara and Robbi Jr. before they possibly ambushed his funeral, but he was no help. He'd traveled to many places and met various people, I was looking for a needle in a haystack.

August 8th, 1998, I returned home from running errands, surprised to see a mixed boy who was a spitting image of Riot in my living room. He introduced himself as Robbi Jr.

Seeing that boy actualized what I hoped wasn't real. After all the fighting, canvassing, protesting, recruiting, imprisonment, and deaths of comrades, Riot chose to sleep with the oppressor."

Ginger stopped drawing on herself. "She was a white woman?"

Sonia didn't respond.

"That night, I woke up to a gunshot. Riot shot himself in the head."

Yvonne smacked on her gum. "Cyrus said you killed him."

"He died from a self-inflicted gunshot wound, and the courts had a field day with my ass. With my extensive history and tumultuous relationship with the injustice system, I was charged for his death. I've been incarcerated for twenty- five years, and seeing what this country has become is sickening.

The interracial relationships, feminine niggas, and bird-brain bitches—there will be no revolution with this dumb-ass generation."

I interceded. "This is the perfect segue for my first question. What life advice would you give younger generations?"

Sonia rolled her eyes. "They need more than advice. They need a hardwire reset to wean them off instant gratification, the drugs and substances that eat at their brain matter, and external validation from degenerates.

I'd encourage my people to take full advantage of this system and its benefits. We were conditioned to believe government assistance was a handicap when, in reality, much government assistance assists in white folks' generational wealth. They use EBT, Section 8, and WIC far more than we do, and we struggle far more than they do.

I'd also remind my people that there is enough for everyone. Enough money, love, land, and resources to stop competing with one another and eliminate the actual enemy.

As for women, I wish we lived our lives like mediocre white men, audacious and selfish. Instead, women are governed by their pride and achievement kinks when no one cares how far you've overextended yourself. Women's shitty boundaries are self-sacrificial, and their mental and physical health continues to suffer.

We must play selfishly in this selfish world. Prioritize your desires, wants, and needs, despite societal and cultural norms. There is no winning for women when a man is involved. You'd be a fool to allow a man to baby momma you, and marriage isn't the safety net we think it is.

As a wife, you will be a victim of infidelity, you will be a single mother in your marriage, and that man can and will leave you whenever you are no longer valuable to him.

It's imperative to have a plan B, your own money, make decisions that serve you first and best, say no more often, and kill men more. History has shown violence is the only way to change the behavior of men. Make them suffer.

I cleared my throat. "What has been your most difficult struggle during your time here?"

Sonia paused, staring at her worn-out slides. "I can't say I have struggled with anything I wouldn't be struggling with on the outside. We're all prisoners of something.

Yes, I would enjoy coming and going as I please, but most people can't comprehend that in this capitalist rat race, we are the rats chasing cheese and frantically pumping productivity to make the white man wealthy.

I am at peace with my decisions and their consequences. I have no regrets. Watchu young heffas say? And that's on period."

The group erupted in laughter.

"Sonia, I appreciate you joining us and sharing your wisdom with us. Everyone did a great job today. I'll see you all tomorrow."

elvis

On the drive home I replayed Sonia's message. Her delivery may have been straightforward, but there was no lie detected.

Women, especially women of color, are the glue that holds families, corporations, and society together but are the most overlooked and underestimated group of people, especially in research.

I thoroughly enjoy working with women in the classrooms and in my research studies. While doing so, I'm often reminded of our strength, beauty, intellect, and kindness.

However, there's a heavy ache I can't ignore when I retract the many involuntary participants that the forefathers of psychology tested on. Most historical research was unethically practiced on impoverished and disease- ridden people of color, by conducting surgeries without anesthesia, dismembering body parts without consent, and intentionally infecting participants. This is a result of white supremacy and their gatekeeping practices to uphold patriarchy, misogyny, and racism.

Very little has changed. My experience with research has been tenacious. Researchers and corporations aren't interested in ethics or inclusion. They want research that confirms their already skewed beliefs about the world around them.

Recovering crash out
Antonia Royal Whitmore

As a double minority, an African American woman, my insights were rarely considered. I was treated as an assistant instead of an equally qualified partner and on a few occasions forced to step down from projects altogether.

Reestablishing my place in the professional world after my release has been anything short of grueling. Researchers are eager to discredit my work and spotlight my criminal record. I've seen researchers attempt to plagiarize my work, incorrectly replicate my projects, and undercut my funding.

Knowing there are countless women who can benefit from the research I am conducting allows me to see these attempts at my reputation as small roadblocks. Women of color deserve a voice in research, and I'm here to ensure those voices are heard.

My train of thought was interrupted by my cellphone ringing.

"Hey, baby. Dinner is on the stove. I'll be back home in a few hours, ready to hear about your day," Elvis greeted.

Elvis and I have been married for a few years. I never considered myself to be a lesbian or a cougar, but I also never considered myself to be a criminal either.

Elvis helped me transition into lockup life. She took me under her wing and was my first participant in my research study. Elvis wasn't a crash out, though. Her story was different. She opened up about the struggles of divorced parents and co-parenting.

Every weekend she spent with her father helping him fix cars. On the weekdays, she cared for her mother as she spiraled into depression and used alcohol to cope.

One day after basketball practice, Elvis's mother picked her up under the influence, which wasn't the first time she'd driven intoxicated. Her mother dozed off behind the wheel and T-boned another vehicle. Elvis was instructed by her mother to switch seats since she was driving under the influence with an expired license.

In most cases, minors received a lesser sentence, but a few days after the accident, the person her mother hit suffered a heart attack and died. Because Elvis admitted she was behind the wheel, she was charged with vehicular manslaughter and spent her 18th birthday behind bars.

When Elvis and I met, she was serving the tail end of her five-year sentence. We started off as two inmates bonding over Law & Order SVU. Eventually she turned into my research recruiter and assistant. Somewhere in the mix, I began to blush when she smiled, my heart skipped a beat when we touched, and I longed to be in her presence every chance I got.

I refused to disclose this to her in fear that my feelings were merely a survival response. I believed that I was only attracted to her because I was lonely and afraid. How else could I, a heterosexual divorcee, be attracted to another woman almost ten years my junior, with no prior interest in women? It truly didn't matter though. What I felt with Elvis was something I'd never experienced with a man. It wasn't sexual but spiritual.

Recovering crash out

Antonia Royal Whitmore

Once she was released, I connected her with my sister Drue to arrange employment and housing as a token of appreciation.

I was shocked that Elvis came to visit me regularly. She eventually expressed her feelings, but I didn't want her to waste any more of her youth on me.

Once I was released, we started dating. She proposed a few months later, and I've never been happier. Memories of her hold me through my day when I'm behind the walls of Hazelwood.

release date

The same uneasy feeling crept up my skin as I pulled up to the prison. My survival instincts were activated at the prison's gates.

When I entered the prison, I couldn't shake the feeling that something was different about today. The air was odd and unstable, cooler than usual. I always wanted to know if the chill atmosphere was an intentional or unintentional layer of punishment. My fingers and toes grew cold, yet my armpits remained moist.

One thing lockup taught me was to befriend my intuition and listen to my body. Anytime I felt something was off, I was correct. I knew to precede the day with caution.

As I headed to my group, the warden called me into his office.

I peeped my head through his door. "Good morning, Warden? How are you doing?"

The warden skipped all pleasantries. "Class is cancelled. You're being shipped to Ashfield Penitentiary."

I stepped further into his office. "Excuse me?" Warden kept his eyes glued on his paperwork.

Recovering crash out
Antonia Royal Whitmore

"Your success with our inmates has attracted other facilities that needed your insight. You've been summoned to Ashfield Penitentiary effective immediately."

My pulse quickened, and the room began to blur. "I'm not an inmate anymore; you can't just transfer me like I'm livestock, like I'm a goddamn slave."

"I don't make the rules, and you agreed to this in your probation contract."

"This class just started. You and I both understand how harmful it is to build trust with inmates. Switching facilitators will decrease the overall success rate of this group. You're putting these women in jeopardy and toying with their freedom."

"This group wasn't going to have a high success rate in the first place."

"Excuse me?"

"Chloe is in the hole."

I took a seat. I could understand Ginger, maybe even Sonia, but Chloe was unbelievable.

"What do you mean she's in the hole? She's not once had an altercation with anyone. What exactly transpired in the last 24 hours?"

"From what I gathered, when her fiancé visited her yesterday, he broke things off with and she didn't take it well. This morning she woke up yelling in a foreign language. She destroyed her cell and tried to take the keys of a correctional officer. She's been in the hole for a few hours and has not spoken a word of English. All she keeps saying is je nes sais pas."

"The breakup triggered her dissociative fugue. Let me see her."

The warden shook his head. "Absolutely not. Your time here has expired. Once you leave these doors, you will no longer be allowed in this facility. That is unless Cupid strikes again."

The warden was right. I knew at any point in time, I could be transferred to a different facility. I was certain my good report at Hazelwood ensured my position, but there was no loyalty for an ex-con.

I walked out of his office with tears gliding my eyelids. I was saddened to abruptly leave the girls, but I knew they could handle their own.

Before I left, I asked the correctional officer to add Omorose and Mademoiselle Inca to Chloe's visitor list. After spending my night searching for Omorose and Mademoiselle Inca, I was able to locate them both and speak with them regarding Chloe. They were baffled by Chloe's fate but more than willing to provide her with love and support.

It was difficult to process that my time at Hazelwood Grove had ended, that my release date was finally here. Despite the anxiety attacks and horrendous stench, Hazelwood was my home.

It wasn't like Stockholm syndrome. I wasn't in love with my captor, but I grew to appreciate the lessons, knowledge, and community I experienced. I'm ashamed to say I became comfortable here, the worst thing anyone should do in a hostile environment. The one thing I will ensure doesn't happen at Ashfield.

I was preparing to enter a different world filled with slimy, manipulative, demons. Or what we call them back at home in Chicago, Goofies.

Unrecoverable goofies.

BOOK II:

UNRECOVERABLE GOOFY

born a goofy

Inmate #34536: "I don't even know why I'm in jail, bruh. That bitch lied on my name and said I put my hands on her. She was just begging me to choke her out when I was in her guts; now I'm an abuser for putting my hands on her?

I hate these shady-ass bitches."

Inmate #56399: "I loved creating masks for each of my victims, pretending to be exactly who they needed me to be to gain their trust. Seeing them relax in my presence made the kill that much sweeter. No sex aroused me more than the screams of a dying woman. The louder she screamed, the harder I got.

I collected body parts from each victim and added them to my collection. Do you think they'll return my collection once I'm released?"

Inmate #98275: "It's her fault. Didn't nobody tell her stupid ass to go through my phone. She hurt her own damn feelings. Her spiteful ass called my probation officer knowing I was going to fail my drug test. I got something for her ass, though."

Inmate #94909: "She told the whole hood I was gay, knowing damn well that was some foo shit. I shot up her momma house, and now her sister gone and she paralyzed. Folks need to keep my name out they mouth.

Recovering crash out

Antonia Royal Whitmore

Inmate #40575: I didn't know you couldn't give a newborn pop. The way that lil nigga swallowed that whole bottle of Dr. Pepper was crazy. The baby started acting weird, so I left that motherfucka in the room for a few days until his momma came back from Jamaica. If she was around to take care of her baby, he wouldn't have died. She blamed me, but all I could say was, bomboclat!"

Inmate #82653: "That ass didn't look like it belonged to a fourteen-year-old, and the look in her eyes said she wanted it. Young hoes got the sweetest pussy, but the best pussy is the one you gotta fight for."

Picking program participants at Ashfield Penitentiary was insufferable. I was completely sick to my stomach listening for hours as men degraded women, excused their despicable behaviors, and confessed to unbelievable crimes.

Nothing prepared me for the low level of thinking, inability to take accountability, victim mentality, and harassment, but I simply didn't have a choice. My probation agreement wasn't up for another two years.

I scheduled a meeting with the prison's warden. "None of these men are fit for my program."

"We'll switch up your program." Were his only words.

He wasn't wrong. There was no room for professionalism at an all-male state prison. It was time to reconnect with who I was before professionalism.

Recovering crash out

Antonia Royal Whitmore

I selected the lesser of evils and began my first class.

"If it were up to me, you motherfuckas would be born in jail, forced to prove yourselves worthy to join the rest of civilization."

Other Books By Antonia Royal Whitmore

Urban Fiction

Nine Inches

Children's literature

Melanin Laughs

You Are: Tu Eres

Boys Wash Their Hands:

Thanksgiving with the Bully

Nubia's Kwanzaa

Treasures of Truth: The Untold Story of St. Patrick's Day

Our Independence Day: A Juneteenth

Coloring Books

Color Me Culture: Adult Coloring

Color Me Culture: Hair Affirmation

Color Me Culture: A Rainbow Journey

Join the tribe

IG: @publacklibrary

Tiktok: @publacklibrary

Website: www.publacklibrary.org

Email: info@publacklibrary.org